INSIDE
The Business of Show

HOW TO CREATE A SUSTAINABLE, PROFESSIONAL ACTING CAREER

Get industry-ready with this companion workbook and the four-class, online video series, *Inside the Business of Show.*

Class 1: *The Business of Acting* with Judy Kain

Class 2: *The Castable Actor* with Tom Burke

Class 3: *How to Break into Broadway* with Christopher Henry Young

Class 4: *The Castable Headshot* with Tom Burke and Kevin McIntyre

ONLINE VIDEO SERIES SOLD SEPARATELY WITH MONEY BACK GUARANTEE

The video series contains more than 50 segments. Go to

https://www.insidethebusinessofshow.com/

or scan the QR code to purchase the complete series or to get

12 FREE VIDEO SEGMENTS

Compiled by Michael Vezo

Westcom Press, LLC
La Quinta, California

Inside the Business of Show:
How To Create A Sustainable, Professional Acting Career

Copyright © 2021 Michael Vezo

Published by:
Westcom Press, LLC
53605 Avenida Cortez
La Quinta, California 92253

https://www.insidethebusinessofshow.com/

contact: producer@insidethebusinessofshow.com
310-406-8300

Published in the United States of America 10 9 8 7 6 5 4 3 2

All rights reserved. No part of this publication may be reproduced, stored in any retrieval system, or transmitted in any form or by any means, mechanical, photocopying, recording, or otherwise, without permission from the publisher.

ISBN: 978-1-938620-85-0

> Educators and agents, contact us to discuss video access subscription rates for your department, college or university, or talent agency:
>
> producer@insidethebusinessofshow.com
> 310-406-8300

How to start and advance your acting career

This workbook organizes and enhances information from a series of more than fifty pre-recorded video segments by entertainment industry professionals. Their presentations uncover valuable inside information, marketing tools, and proven strategies to help actors start, restart, or kick start and maintain a career in film, stage, TV, and commercials.

Here are your class presenters

Judy Kain has been a professional actress, public speaker, and teacher for 40 years, showcasing her skills and talents in more than 400 commercials and 125 roles for film and television. At her **Keep It Real Acting Studios** in North Hollywood, CA her success as a teacher has lead to numerous awards. Her successful book, *I Booked It! The Commercial Actors Handbook, and h*er in-depth video *The Business of Acting* inspired this class list and workbook.

Tom Burke is a premier image consultant and branding expert. He transitioned from a successful international print and runway model to an accomplished on-camera actor, then to a proficient on-set acting consultant and a headshot coach. He has the rare talent and keen eye to successfully help actors pinpoint their specific types, brands, and most marketable images. His column for *Backstage* helps actors understand the importance of packaging their marketable branded image.

Christopher Henry Young is a Broadway actor, singer, and dancer, most recently appearing in Hamilton. His first role was in a high-school production of *Beauty and the Beast*, and it sparked his enduring love for musicals. On his way to Broadway, his experience included theme park performances, cruise ships, and regional theatre contracts. As he grew as an artist, he worked with forward-thinking actors and creative teams who encouraged him to continuing striving for new goals. He generously shares what he's learned along the way in his bio and his video lectures.

Kevin McIntyre, photographer, has a background as a successful actor and musical performer, which gives him a unique understanding of actors' needs. He's been a headshot photographer in Los Angeles and in Canada for nearly 25 years, specializing in natural-light photography. His notable clients include Oscar winners Octavia Spenser and Mo'nique, as well as Ken Jeong, Eva Mendes, and Kendall Jenner. In order to maximize an actor's impact on online casting sites, Kevin ensures his clients get a portfolio showing their range and their brand. They leave his studio confident their headshots will work.

*Imagination means nothing
without doing.*

—Charlie Chaplin

Foreword

In 2019, Rami Malek won the Academy Award for best actor with his outstanding performance in *Bohemian Rhapsody* as Freddie Mercury, the iconic lead singer for the rock band Queen.

A 2003 graduate of the theatre program at the University of Evansville, Rami had more than enough talent to book work in Hollywood. However, in a recent interview with Terry Gross of National Public Radios's *Fresh Air*, he told of his early years in Hollywood, living with his parents and working in a restaurant delivering falafel and pizzas. Along with the food he'd deliver a manila envelope stuffed with his headshot and résumé to any customer he thought could help him break into Hollywood. As an actor with no agent and who wasn't a member of the Screen Actors Guild, he had to rely on his own marketing efforts to charm his way into an audition.

Rami Malek obviously made it. His talent, training, persistence, and tireless marketing eventually opened doors and got him to the top. But the same predicament facing him nearly twenty years ago still exists: How do actors learn to leverage their talent in order to book jobs in the competitive entertainment industry?

That is exactly why these video classes and workbook were created.

The workbook and its video lectures will help you launch, re-launch, or kickstart your acting career and will give you encouragement and momentum to help keep that career moving forward. The four video classes, with more than fifty segments, provide valuable information delivered by successful industry professionals. They offer insight into auditions, casting directors, agents, and producers, in order to help you become industry-savvy. You'll come away with information to help you market and run your acting career as a successful business.

This is not drama school; this is about the real world where the competition is greater than ever. If you funnel some of the energy you spend on improving your acting and performance skills into learning and utilizing the information in these video classes you'll discover your castable self, your brand, and how to leverage them as a successful professional. I guarantee you will uncover valuable nuggets throughout these video classes and in this workbook that will help you stand out in the crowd and move you forward in your career.

Break a leg!

Michael Vezo
Producer
Inside the Business of Show

Table of Contents

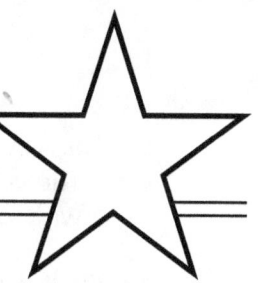

The Class Presenters iii
Foreword v
Helpful Links xii

CLASS 1: *THE BUSINESS OF ACTING* with Judy Kain 1

   1. *Introduction to Judy Kain's The Business of Acting* 3
      Judy Kain introduces The Business of Acting course with a discussion of first impressions. Make yours a great one to benefit your acting career.

   2. *Be Prepared, Part 1* 7
      Liftoff with proven strategies, tools, and tips.

   3. *Be Prepared, Part 2* 13
      More tools and tips to help you stand out to casting directors, agents, and other important connections.

   4. *How to Get More Auditions* 19
      How do you see yourself and how do others see you? Judy Kain expands on the importance of strategically getting your name out there.

   5. *How to Find a Good Photographer* 23
      Avoid making mistakes with your headshot. It's your most important marketing tool.

   6. *Uploading Headshots onto Casting Websites* 27
      Judy Kain discusses professional casting sites where you upload your headshots plus more online resources.

   7. *Postcards* 29
      The enduring power of postcards—an affordable way to get your name, face, and brand out there.

   8. *Gifts and Thank You Notes* 31
      Judy Kain covers when and how to send a gift or thank-you note. Learn the special "win-win-win" strategy.

   9. *Business Cards* 35
      Judy Kain walks you through creative ways to make your business card a powerful, strategic, marketing tool.

  10. *Showcases* 39
      Showcases are part of an actor's overall branding and networking.

  11. *You Are Responsible For Your Career* 41
      "My agent isn't getting me out" —and more complaints that need to be solved by YOU.

12. ***The Actor's Team*** 45
    The value of agents, and the importance of choosing an agency that aligns with who you are.

13. ***Finding an Agent*** 47
    How to find an agent, and effective methods to prevent your mailed submission from being tossed with the junk mail.

14. ***The Agency Interview*** 51
    Surprising advice from Judy Kain on how to conduct yourself as you drive the interview.

15. ***Self-Taping*** 53
    Guidelines for making a professional, stand-out audition tape.

16. ***SlateShots*sm*** 55
    This inexpensive, relatively new tool increases your chances to be called for an audition. Judy Kain shows how seven seconds can have an impact.

17. ***Social Media: The New Calling Card*** 57
    Leverage your personal social media presence to strengthen your brand in a professional and engaged manner.

About Judy Kain 59

CLASS 2: THE CASTABLE ACTOR with Tom Burke 61

1. ***Are You Castable?*** 63
    Tom Burke introduces you to what "castable" means and helps you to understand the film and TV business and how they work.

2. **Creating and Presenting a *Marketable Image*** 65
    Trying to be what you think a casting director wants will not open any doors. Tom Burke teaches that it all starts with three words: Honest, Realistic, Specific.

3. ***Type*** 67
    Learn what ***type*** is and the difference between type and type of roles. Once you learn your type embrace it, own it, present it.

4. ***Marketability*** 69
    Tom Burke explains the different categories that fit a type. When you know what roles are right for you, you can target them.

5. ***Brand - Part I*** 71
    No one is looking for generic! Tom Burke helps you focus on what is special and unique about you.

6. ***Brand - Part II*** 73
    Use your friends and family to nail down your brand and dispel what's left of your generic image.

7. ***Headshots - Five Common Mistakes*** 75
   Learn the four most important jobs your headshots do for you. And more importantly... are your headshots living up to the task?

8. ***Course Wrap Up, Now What?*** 77
   While wrapping up, Tom shares even more professional expertise and more specific strategies to help separate you from the crowd.

9. ***Castable Conclusions*** 79
   You need to know who you are, where you fit, and what you offer that is unique and special. Being talented or having a "look" isn't enough; you need to present as a marketable, castable actor at all times so that casting directors, agents, managers, etc. know exactly who you are and what they can do with you. It's easier than you think!

About Tom Burke 81

CLASS 3: How To Break Into Broadway with Christopher Henry Young..........................83

1. ***Introduction*** 85
   Christopher introduces the exciting world of the professional stage performer, and why a successful career is attainable!

2. ***Preparation, Part One*** 87
   Why your headshots need to really show your personality, and the importance of an up-to-date résumé that includes all credits.

3. ***Preparation, Part Two*** 89
   Learn what you need to bring to an audition. Christopher explains why you prepare an audition book, why you need to memorize a "song in the style of show," and how to work with the accompanist.

4. ***Stage Skills*** 91
   Christopher discusses how to assess your skills and how to prepare those skills before an audition. You'll also learn what to bring to an audition.

5. ***Classes and Training*** 93
   Christopher discusses the importance of taking classes and what types of classes to take in order to keep up with the demands of a professional career.

6. ***Auditions*** 95
   Are casting calls and auditions the same thing? Christopher guides you through how to find auditions, what information you need to know from a casting notice, and more!

7. ***Self-Care*** 97
   So often, self-care is overlooked, especially when zipping from one audition to the next. Yet it's a critical component of becoming a professional stage performer who works long hours. Specific warm up exercises are demonstrated by Christopher in this very important aspect of your career.

8. ***Nutritional Approach to a Broadway Body*** 99
   Do a cheeseburger and fries factor into a healthy diet to help you get through the challenging days of auditions, rehearsals, and performances?

9. ***At-Home Warm-Up, Section 1, Cardio*** 101
   Christopher introduces his Basic At-Home Warm-Up which goes way beyond basic stretching. In these next three videos the Warm-Ups includes cardio, rotating your joints, and your core, as well as lower and upper body exercises. They get you going and create the strength you need to be an onstage performer.

10. ***At-Home Warm-Up, Sections 2 & 3, Joints*** 103
    Christopher continues The Basic At-Home Warm-Up with emphasis on warming up your joints and lower body.

11. ***At-Home Warm-Up, Sections 4 & 5, Core*** 105
    Sections 4 & 5 include building core muscles through plank position and warming up your upper body with arm, shoulder, and chest exercises.

12. ***You Booked A Show, Now What*** 107
    You made it through the audition and call backs, now you need to understand the importance of knowing the show's creative materials and being ready for the physical demands of rehearsals. In this segment you'll also learn about other acting parts of a prodcution that can expand your experience and career.

13. ***Professionalism*** 109
    Survive the audition like a pro: The importance of being prepared, knowing rehearsal etiquette, and "notes" from the creative team.

14. ***Equity and Non-Equity*** 111
    An explanation of Actors' Equity Association, and the advantages and disadvantages of membership.

15. ***Common Mistakes*** 113
    Christopher warns against hiring an agent or manager too soon in your career, and he urges you to cultivate your unique characteristics rather than compare yourself to others.

16. ***Career Longevity*** 115
    Keeping up with the ever-evolving world of theater, staying calm and collected, and preventing a premature end to your career.

17. ***Course Wrap Up and Conclusions*** 117
    Christopher provides some last words of encouragement reminding you that the business is changing daily and there's so much opportunity than ever to have a stage career you love!

About Christopher Henry Young 119

CLASS 4: The Castable Headshot with Tom Burke & Kevin McIntyre 121

1. ***Know Who You Are*** 123
   You must first establish who you are; put some work into preparation. Whether it's your first time getting headshots taken, or your 10th time, it's extremely important to ask yourself some important questions before booking a headshot session, such as "What's my type?", and more.

2. ***Finding a Photographer*** 125
   You need to find the right photographer for *YOU*. Tom Burke provides very experienced strategies and tips on how to find a photographer that fits your personality type and your goals for the shoot. Also, how to discuss exactly where a photographer actually does their shoots in order to give the actor an overall comfort and safety level before the shoot.

3. ***The Cost of Your Headshot Session*** 127
   The cost of a headshot session can vary. You need to approach and analyze the costs as a professional; i.e., a low price is not always a deal, and likewise, spending a fortune on headshots doesn't always get you the shots you need either. Tom Burke gives you a perspective on how to approach this important aspect of your career.

4. ***Bring Emotion to the Headshot Session*** 129
   Tom Burke addresses *how to innately bring emotion to each shot*, so that it's the *real* you who is experiencing the moment in the camera. Bringing specific emotion (not contrived) to different shots helps you stand out among the competition.

5. ***What Makes a Good Headshot and a Bad Headshot*** 131
   Plan a portfolio of headshots showing your range. Learn how to connect with the camera.

6. ***Q & A from the Photographer's Viewpoint*** 133
   In this Q & A, photographer Kevin McIntyre provides actors some insight into what makes a terrific shoot from the photographer's point of view.

7. ***Arrive at the Studio*** 135
   Tom Burke and Kevin McIntyre provide details about your clothing/uniform choices and give professional perspective about the controversial topic of whether to bring a hair and makeup person. Their experience, insight, and guidance helps you to present the *professional you*.

8. ***Headshot Session Demonstration*** 137
   Finally! The headshot session in action. Tom Burke and Kevin McIntyre go through several valuable tips and show you the do's and don'ts during a productive, mock headshot session.

9. ***Now What? Post Photo Session Process*** 139
   Tom Burke and Kevin McIntyre go through the process of the post-photo-shoot session. As the photographer, Kevin lays out what his process is before delivering the photos. Tom and Kevin discuss choosing photos that adhere to the four major jobs each photo must do...and why it's so important NOT to do this by yourself!

About Tom Burke and About Kevin McIntyre...141

Helpful Links

Below are links found within the workbook pages of *Inside the Business of Show*:

In order of appearance

Inside the Business of Show Webpage i
https://www.insidethebusinessofshow.com/

AUDITIONS and CASTING 11, 40

AuditionsFree
http://www.auditionsfree.com/

CastingAbout
https://www.castingabout.com/

ActorsAccess
https://www.actorsaccess.com/

AGENTS 45, 48

The Association of Talent Agents
https://www.agentassociation.com/index.php?submenu=MemberCompanies&src=membership

IMDb (Pro) 46
https://help.imdb.com/article/imdbpro/membership-benefits/pro-tips-for-talent/GHQ5W5C2BJ2KWP77?ref_=helpart_nav_4#

SAG/AFTRA: SCREEN ACTORS GUILD/AMERICAN FEDERATION OF TELEVISION AND RADIO ARTISTS 46
https://www.sagaftra.org/about

SELF-CARE:

Vocal WarmUp 97
https://www.musicnotes.com/now/tips/enhance-your-voice-with-these-vocal-warmups-and-breathing-exercises/
NOTE: If you receive a 404 error message, go to the search tool on the MusicNotes page and type, "breathing exercises".

Diet and Nutrition 100

Ideal Meal Plan https://www.livestrong.com/article/443807-ideal-meal-plan/

Healthy Diet for Dancers https://www.liveabout.com/healthy-diet-for-dancers-1006899

Healthy Snack Options https://www.pointemagazine.com/healthy-food-for-dancers-2565527028.html

FitForBroadway https://www.fitforbroadway.com/

ACTORS EQUITY 111
https://www.actorsequity.org/

CLASS 1

The Business of Acting
with Judy Kain

Judy Kain

Notes

CLASS 1: THE BUSINESS OF ACTING

Introduction to The Business of Acting

Before you watch Video 1 — Introduction to The Business of Acting

Introductions and first impressions are important. Before you meet someone in the industry for the first time, take a look at yourself and do a character self-evaluation. How are you sitting? What are you wearing? What do your backpack or the other items you're carrying say about you? What do you think someone will infer about you during this first-time meeting . . . especially if this is an "industry" introduction?

Keep It Real

Why are you watching these workshop videos? What do you hope to learn? Describe a goal you can work toward as you watch these videos—a goal that will make this a valuable experience for you. If you don't have a final answer right now, just jot down some ideas—we'll come back to this after watching the first video.

Watch Video 1: Introduction

While you watch the video:

Take note of what stands out to you the first time you watch each video. Do not write down a full transcript of what's being said; use this space to jot down your initial impressions. Do this with every video in the library.

After you watch the video:

What's a casting director's number one complaint?

Read the following paragraph from the Internal Revenue Service and underline the aspects that make something a business.

> A trade or business is generally an activity carried on for a livelihood or in good faith to make a profit. The facts and circumstances of each case determine whether or not an activity is a trade or business. The regularity of activities and transactions and the production of income are important elements. You do not need to actually make a profit to be in a trade or business as long as you have a profit motive. You do need, however, to make ongoing efforts to further the interests of your business.

CLASS 1: THE BUSINESS OF ACTING

How is acting a business? Use this chart to help organize your ideas:

Aspects of a business e.g. budgeting, marketing, planning	Why you need to manage this as an actor

Now, assess where you are in the audition process. Draw on your past audition and performance experiences and answer the following questions:

Keep It Real

What's working for you right now? How are auditions going? Have you been pleased with the roles you've been getting?

Keep It Real

Revisit the goal you set for yourself before watching the video. Is there anything about it you would like to change? Remember, the purpose of this goal is for you to make these workshop videos a valuable experience for *you* specifically.

Judy Kain

Notes

CLASS 1: THE BUSINESS OF ACTING

Be Prepared, Part 1

Before you watch Video 2 — Be Prepared, Part 1

Imagine you are talking to a friend who has never been to a job interview, and they ask what they should do to prepare for it. What advice would you give them?

Imagine you are talking to someone who has never auditioned before, and they ask you what they should do to prepare before they present their first audition. What advice would you give them?

Keep It Real

What does preparing for an audition look like for you? Has there ever been an audition for which you felt fully prepared? Why or why not? What are some areas where you tend to be weak in preparation? What are some steps you could take to be more prepared?

Watch Video 2: Be Prepared, Part 1

While you watch the video:

What facts made the biggest impression on you?

After you watch the video:

As an actor, do you believe you are prepared for auditions?

What did you learn that will help you achieve your personal goal?

Class 1: The Business of Acting

Judy Kain recommends a comprehensive list of items to keep in your car so you're always prepared for an audition. Watch the beginning of the video again and jot that list in the left column. Next to each item, check whether it's something you already have in your car, already own but need to put in your car, or you need to buy. Research the costs and add prices at the right; total them at the bottom for a good estimate of the cost of preparing your car for an audition. *(If you don't currently have a car, imagine that you do; all of your answers will be "move to car" or "need to buy")*

Item	Already in Car	Move to car	Need to buy	Cost
	☐	☐	☐	
	☐	☐	☐	
	☐	☐	☐	
	☐	☐	☐	
	☐	☐	☐	
	☐	☐	☐	
	☐	☐	☐	
	☐	☐	☐	
	☐	☐	☐	
	☐	☐	☐	
Total Cost				

Keep It Real

Some actors actually walk into auditions without knowing why they are there ("My agent just told me to come"). There's no need for ignorance; a good casting notice will tell you the name of a project, its classification, the time of the audition, the location of the audition, and how it will be conducted. Judy Kain explains why you will have an advantage knowing the facts about each audition.

In the space on the next page, fill in as much as you remember about casting notices. Then, re-watch the video and fill in as much of the "why" as you can. You can also use the space to reflect about yourself and why understanding these elements would matter to you specifically.

Before you head into an audition, *why* is it important to know the following:

★ The name of the project and the classification? (Is it a film, TV show, commercial, industrial voiceover, print job, pilot or ongoing show, low budget, ultra-low budget, deferred payment?)

★ The time of the audition?

★ The location of the audition?

★ Who will you read for?

★ How it will be conducted?

Keep It Real

It's important to read all the lines on a casting notice and make the most of the information you learn. As a working, professional actor, your agent will send you casting notices and will help you schedule auditions. For now, head to http://www.auditionsfree.com/ and find a casting call for an intriguing audition. (Many of these auditions may also be closer to where you live than you'd expect!) Can you find all of the information that Judy Kain describes? Choose an audition (near or far) and pull out the information reviewed in the above questions. How would you use that information to prepare for that specific audition?

Judy Kain

Notes

CLASS 1: THE BUSINESS OF ACTING

Be Prepared, Part 2

Before you watch Video 3 — Be Prepared, Part 2

1. Review the goal you created for yourself during the introduction segment?

2. Before you watch "Be Prepared, Part 2" – review Part 1. What elements of preparation did Judy Kain highlight in the video? What stood out?

3. Film acting has its own special vocabulary. Write your definition of the following terms before you watch Part II:

    ★ Casting Notice

    ★ Sides

    ★ Copy

    ★ Eyeline

Watch Video 3: Be Prepared, Part 2

While you watch the video:

What facts made the biggest impression on you?

After you watch the video:

What did you learn that will help you achieve your personal goal?

★ Practice! How can you make this advice apply to you?

Practice *not* miming.

Sit as if you are at a tea party. How could you act the following lines without miming or without bringing your own tea cup and cookies?

> "Mmm. Just the right temperature! Ah, Betsy, you always remember exactly how I like my tea. And are those little cookies? Oh, you must let me have one! Oh, thank you! Mmm, delicious."

Practice using your sides as a prop

Rehearse the previous scene with your lines (your "sides") written on a piece of paper. Use it as a prop in the scene (but not a teacup or a cookie). How does having your sides as a prop enhance the scene?

CLASS 1: THE BUSINESS OF ACTING

Practice reflective listening

Watch the video again and use reflective listening to repeat all the directions that you hear while you're watching. How does this change your experience of watching the video? How can you do this in an audition without annoying the casting director?

Practice saying "let me do another" in a polite way.

You need to use a confident tone that isn't demanding, begging, or whining. Record yourself saying "let me do another" in your own words, and then review the clip. Evaluate your efforts, and revise them.

Keep It Real

How can you keep your hair out of your face in an attractive way? Practice two or three techniques in the mirror or with a friend. Take photos to use later for reference.

Keep It Real

Absorb the following audition preparation advice and think about how it can apply to you? Suggested reflection questions follow some of the advice topics.

★ Prepare your body! How can you make this advice apply to you?

Work out, stretch, do some breathing before the audition. What quick warmups do you like? What stretches help you feel limber and ready to move? Write these down so that you can refer to them before an audition. (Never ever do warmups at the audition site!)

Use eye drops. Have you ever used eye drops before? Do you know anyone who has? Why would eye drops matter for working in film? Why would the day of your audition be a bad time to use eye drops for the first time?

Shower and use deodorant. On screen, people can't smell you. Why is it still important to shower/wear deodorant?

Don't wear fragrance. If it's important to smell nice, why should you NOT wear fragrance?

Hair out of the way What is the point of a film audition if they can't see your face?

★ **Prepare your mind!** How can you make this advice apply to you?

Focus Have you done any acting games or breathing exercises that help you focus?

Pay Attention. What distractions could you eliminate before heading into the rehearsal room?

Memorize your part the day before your audition. What techniques help you memorize quickly? What physical cues help you get into character?

★ **Prepare your craft!** How can you make this advice apply to you?

Learn your camera angles. Do you know what your camera angles are? If not, what steps will you take to learn them?

Don't be too big. What does that mean to you? What makes it tempting to be "too big"? What techniques can you use for grounding yourself?

Take improv classes so you feel comfortable playing with the copy.

"The camera picks up desperation… so don't be desperate."

CLASS 1: THE BUSINESS OF ACTING

No miming If you're not allowed to mime, what are you going to do with your hands?

Use your sides as a prop (always, even if you have it memorized)

★ Prepare for interacting! How can you make this advice apply to you?

Reflective listening: listen and repeat the directions you're given.

Don't be afraid to ask questions. What kind of questions could you possibly have during an audition? What would make you feel nervous to ask them?

Ask, "Where's my eyeline?"

If you mess up the copy, just finish and then when they say cut, say "let me do another"

Practice being polite. (Please, thank you, etc.)

DON'T SHAKE ANYONE'S HAND!

Don't prepare in the room—come in ready to work (no warm-ups or breathing in the room).

Be excited if you're asked to prepare something new—take as much time as you need. We often think that if we get ready quickly, the director will be impressed, but this isn't the case. What matters is how well you nail it.

What three steps will you plan to take in approaching new sides so that you can be confident that you're fully prepared?

Don't make excuses—own your audition, thank them, and go about your day.

Judy Kain

Notes

CLASS 1: THE BUSINESS OF ACTING

How To Get More Auditions

Before you watch Video 4 — How To Get More Auditions

Review the goal you created for yourself during the introduction segment and jot down how the previous video segments may have changed your thinking about your career.

This video focuses on the promotion and marketing aspects of your business. Think of some companies that sell to you in your day-to-day life. What effective tactics do they use? How can an actor adopt their marketing tactics to generate more auditions?

Company Name	Promotion Tactics	How to apply those tactics to your career

Watch Video 4: How To Get More Auditions

While you watch the video:

Use this space to jot down your initial impressions and any thoughts or feelings you have while watching.

After you watch the video:

You vs. your castable self. Judy Kain talks about the probable difference between your "castable self" and your true self. Do you find this is true for you?

Keep It Real

To promote and market a product well, you first need to thoroughly understand the product. In this case **you** are the product and it's now time to identify who **you** are!

What's my age range?

What "type" am I?

What are my jobs?

What is my "essence?"

CLASS 1:: THE BUSINESS OF ACTING

What I am most likely to be cast as?

What "bookable uniforms" should I have?

What people in my life bring out these qualities in me:

    Competitiveness

    Honesty

    My flirty side

    My edgy side

    My desire to please

Keep It Real

Create a complete scenario for your headshot shoot.

Judy Kain

Notes

CLASS 1: THE BUSINESS OF ACTING

How To Find a Good Photographer

Before you watch Video 5 — How To Find a Good Photographer

What do you hope to specifically learn from this video segment?

Get your headshot; if you don't have one, find another picture you like.

How old is this picture?

Find specific elements of the photo you like. Use specific vocabulary from the last video to describe this picture.

Write down what you think could be some key differences between a good photo and an industry headshot.

Does this picture represent your castable self?

Watch Video 5: How To Find a Good Photographer

While you watch the video:

Jot down your initial impressions and any thoughts or feelings you have while watching.

After you watch the video:

Search for headshots of at least three actors whom you know. List them below and provide your analysis of the pictures; write down your comments about lighting, backgrounds, etc., and whether you believe the photographer captured the actors' essence.

Ask these actors to share their photographer's name, then follow up: Contact the photographers, talk with them and see who makes you feel comfortable.

Keep It Real

Prepare two more scenarios for your headshot session using the material from Video 4, **How to Get More Auditions**. Develop the scene for your castable self and one of the people you identified who bring out various emotions in you.

Scenario #1

Scenario #2

Keep It Real

Look at the photo of yourself again or at your current headshot. Analyze it with regard to what about it works and what doesn't?

What works?	What doesn't?

Notes

CLASS 1: THE BUSINESS OF ACTING

Uploading Headshots onto Casting Websites

Before you watch Video 6 – Uploading Headshots onto Casting Websites

List any and all casting websites where your headshot is currently posted:

List any other casting websites where you also could post your headshot:

On which social media have you posted your headshot?

Watch Video 6: Uploading Head Shots on Casting Sites

While you watch the video:

Take note of any sites Judy Kain mentions that you haven't already listed above

After you watch the video:

Learn the ins and out of these terms:
- high-rez and low-rez digital photos
- color correction and how it differs from retouching.

Judy mentions that photos should offer a sneak peak into the roles for which you might be cast. Do you have different looks and outfits in your portfolio?

Keep It Real

The last thing you want is to have a generic look and become invisible among the other 2,999 audition hopefuls. You want to fit the type, but add your own personality and style. Keep this thought in mind throughout the selection and audition process and even after you get the booking.

Notes

CLASS 1: THE BUSINESS OF ACTING

Postcards

Before you watch Video 7 – Postcards

Take a moment to reflect and comment on the following statements:

In today's digital world, what is the value of something tangible?

Why do you think companies still use post cards as marketing tools?

Watch Video 7: Postcards

While you watch the video:

As you watch the video, jot down milestones and happy events of the last year that could justify a postcard (new skills, new role, new agent or manager, a holiday, photogenic new pet, finishing classes, etc.).

After you watch the video:

Keep It Real

What is my goal for sending a postcasrd? What results do I expect by sending it?

Once you've nailed down your goal, develop your mailing list. List 20 contacts here.

Postcard recipients	

Before you can get started with the design, you need to choose one of the events you listed earlier to celebrate.

Keep your event, goal, and contacts in mind as you write the copy; it should be fun to read and reflect your personality. What illustrations and information should the postcard include?

Don't forget to include your name, headshot, and contact information.

CLASS 1: THE BUSINESS OF ACTING

Gifts and Thank-You Notes

Before you watch Video — 8 Gifts and Thank-You Notes

When in your daily life have you given and received thank-you notes? Think of a few occasions where thank-you notes are appropriate or important.

As an actor, who do you think-you might need to thank? Why is it important to thank people?

How will understanding who and how you should thank help you achieve your goal set at the beginning of this course?

Watch Video 8: Gifts and Thank-You Notes

After you watch the video:

As an actor, whom do you need to thank? Why? What are the different levels of thanks that you could express to people for different contributions?

Keep It Real

Delivering gifts or gift baskets is not only a great approach to show appreciation to casting directors/producers but also a fabulous way to gain facetime. Use the chart below to estimate the financial investment you'd need to make in creating your thank-you basket. You can use Judy Kain's examples mentioned in the video as well as your own ideas.

Item	Cost
Empty basket	

It's not the cost of the gift that counts; it's that you deliver it in person. A personal touch has a more lasting effect. —Judy Kain

How do I write a good thank you note? Here's a suggested format.

    Dear (Identify a specific recipient),

    Thank you for [insert service here]

    Mention 2-3 specific reasons why that person's work or the work of someone on their staff (story, style of teaching materials, displays, help, etc.) contributed positively to your experience at the event.

    Explain briefly how the overall experience enhanced your life; if you had a connection with them, remind them.

    Close: Sincerely, With Thanks, Gratefully, etc.
    Your full name (and your headshot)

CLASS 1: THE BUSINESS OF ACTING

EXAMPLE:

Dear Mr. Evans,

Thank you for inviting me to the networking luncheon for new actors.

I really liked that you were attentive to the new members of the group and how you made sure everyone had a chance to share. The luncheon not only helped me network and meet new contacts, but also made me feel less alone in the "big city."

Thank you again for inviting me.

Sincerely,

Alice Adams
AliceA@AliceAdams.com

What was good about this thank you note?

What could be improved?

Your turn! Think of someone who you could thank and write a thank you note including all the elements mentioned above.

Notes

CLASS 1: THE BUSINESS OF ACTING

Business Cards

Before you watch Video 9 – Business Cards

Describe your current business card. Is the headshot current? Is it two-sided?

How many cards do you hand out each week and to whom?

Watch Video 9: Business Cards

After you watch the video:
Keep It Real

If cards aren't a big part of your marketing strategy, why not?

How many additional cards do you now plan to hand out each week?

Update your business card.

There are two sides to a card—use them both to market yourself. Be sure to include some extra information to make yourself stand out.

Front of your new business card	
Current information	**To be added**

Back of your new business card	
Current information	**To be added**

CLASS 1: THE BUSINESS OF ACTING

Make a list of contacts who haven't received your business card and should get your new card right away.

People who should have your card (and don't)	

Keep It Real

Buy a good-looking new card case to keep your cards crisp and your card presentation fumble-free.

Notes

CLASS 1: THE BUSINESS OF ACTING

Showcases

Before you watch Video 10 — Showcases

Use the space below to write about your knowledge of showcases . If you've participated in some, write how helpful they have been in regard to advancing your career.

Watch Video 10: Showcases

After you watch the video:

Keep It Real

Because she does not recommend cold-read showcases, Judy Kain encourages you to attend showcases with a prepared scene. Use this space to brainstorm a few scenes that you feel would highlight your acting in a way that could be a positive networking tool at a showcase. After making that list, choose one and commit to learning and developing it in preparation for a showcase.

Judy Kain suggests two websites as ways to find showcase and workshop opportunities. Review each site and make a list of the pros and cons of each one.

CastingAbout.com	https://www.castingabout.com/
Pros	Cons

ActorsAccess.com	https://www.actorsaccess.com/
Pros	Cons

Keep It Real

It's risky to do a cold scene. Get coached professionally before appearing at a showcase. Bring the audience an impression they haven't seen before!

CLASS 1: THE BUSINESS OF ACTING

You Are Responsible for Your Career

Before you watch Video 11 — You Are Responsible for Your Career

What responsibilities should an actor assume to further their career? Make a list of these responsibilities (beyond keeping an updated résumé and cover letter).

Watch Video 11: You Are Responsible for Your Career

While you watch the video:

Complete the following sentence and focus on this thought during the playing of the video:

No one cares more about getting you work than _____ _____ .

Jot down ideas from the video that will help you reach the goal you established at the beginning of the workbook.

After you watch the video:

Keep It Real

★ What have you done for your career today... yesterday?

★ What do you plan to do for your career tomorrow?

★ What have you done for your agent recently?

★ How can you make your agent's job easier?

Judy Kain asks you to consider the following questions regarding your relationship with your agent. Assuming you have an agent, use the prompts below for reflection. (If you don't have an agent, prepare to develop that relationship while keeping these questions in mind):

★ *What information have you already given your agent in order to help you get an audition?*

★ *What information should you be getting ready to give your agent in order to help you get an audition?*

Keep It Real

Once again, revisit the goal that you set for yourself at the beginning of the course. Based on what you've learned so far, what are the next steps can you take to help you reach your goal?

Keep It Real

Judy Kain clearly states that "Money cannot be an issue or an excuse" – and yet beginning an acting career can be expensive.

In this course we've discussed hiring photographers, acting coaches, and renting studio space to film audition footage. Showcases, postcards, and thank you gifts are additional expenses, not to mention housing and transportation costs.

These expenses are also capital investments in your future, just like going to college, acting school, or starting any other type of business.

Knowing the expenses you will incur will make it easier to plan your finances. It'll also make actually spending that money less stressful, and you'll find it easier to follow Judy Kain's advice: "Decide that you will have enough! Decide that you will make it happen!"

Make a list of the expenses discussed in The Business of Acting video series and get a realistic estimate of the expected costs.

Expense Item	Cost

Notes

CLASS 1: THE BUSINESS OF ACTING

The Actor's Team

Before you watch Video 12 — The Actor's Team

Do you need an agent and/or manager? Before you watch the video, think about what you know about the role of a talent agency or a business manager. Answer the following questions to the best of your ability – don't worry about getting it "wrong" – you're trying to provide yourself with a baseline of knowledge.

★ What does an agent and/or manager do?

★ What are the advantages of working with an agent and/or manager?

★ What's the difference between a commercial and a theatrical agent?

★ How has the digital age leveled the playing field?

★ What do you think is the most important characteristic of a good agent for you?

NOTE: The Association of Talent Agents (ATA) is the official trade association of talent agencies across the U.S.A. The list of members along with their web address, physical address, and phone number can be found at:

https://www.agentassociation.com/index.php?submenu=MemberCompanies&src=membership

Watch Video 12: The Actor's Team

While you watch the video:

Judy Kain says to succeed in an acting career in film and television, you need an agent; but, what makes a good agent? Write down what you should look for when recruiting an agent for your actor's team and listen for the critical element your agent must possess.

After you watch the video:

Judy Kain talks about different agencies that represent different types of actors. Based on all of the work you've done to discover your type, figure out which agency you'd like to represent you. Research talent agencies and record below at least three of them and why they'd be a good match for you. (Yes, this will take a while.)

Keep It Real

Who is currently part of your "actor's team"? Family, friends, professional network, other supporters? Make a list of the people on your team and what their role is.

In addition to the list of agents, mentioned on the previous page, as they build their career needs to be aware of two other very important areas of the business: **IMDb (PRO)** and **SAG/AFTRA (The Screen Actors Guild/ American Federation of Television and Radio Artists}.** Here are links that can help you research each organization:

IMDb: https://help.imdb.com/article/imdbpro/membership-benefits/pro-tips-for-talent/GHQ5W5C2BJ2KWP77?ref_=helpart_nav_4#

SAG/AFTRA: https://www.sagaftra.org/about

CLASS 1: THE BUSINESS OF ACTING

Finding an Agent

Before you watch Video 13 — Finding an Agent

What is the goal you created for yourself during the introduction segment of this workbook? How can learning about finding an agent help you make progress toward that goal? If your initial goal has been modified or expanded, can you explain why?

Keep It Real

Before you seek out an agent, you need to make sure you have a solid headshot and résumé.

Take a look at your current headshot. Has it been updated since you learned about headshots in the earlier video? If so, what changes did you make? Do you think the new headshot is stronger? If not, what changes do you need to make? What specifically are you hoping to highlight in your new headshot?

Look at your acting résumé. Does it communicate your type? Your strengths? Compare it to the sample résumés downloadable via this segment's video portal. What might you add to or delete from your résumé so that it aligns better to who you are as an actor and to industry standards?

Watch Video 13: Finding an Agent

While you watch the video:

Judy Kain discusses different types of people in your network who could potentially serve as referrals for agents. While you watch, write down the names of people you know in those roles who could help refer you to a talent agent. (Focus on coaches, casting directors, successful actors.)

Take note of the approach discussed in this video about how to mail your information to an agent.

NOTE: The Association of Talent Agents (ATA) is the official trade association of talent agencies across the U.S.A. The list of members along with their web address, physical address, and phone number can be found at:

https://www.agentassociation.com/index.php?submenu=MemberCompanies&src=membership

After you watch the video:

Keep It Real

How would a postcard that you'd send to a talent agent differ from the postcard you designed in the earlier lesson?

What suggestion does Judy Kain give you to set yourself apart from other submissions?

Here's an example of a cover letter to an agent:

Dear [insert name here]

"I was referred by…" or "[Name] suggested I contact you"

"I just … [accomplishment, class, etc.]" (Hint: you're about to finish Judy Kain's course!) "and I would love to meet you. Please let me know when we could schedule an appointment."

Thank you, etc.

Sincerely,

[Your Name]

Use the above example to draft your own cover letter.

Then formulate a plan to create the other elements you need that will set you apart from other prospective clients who are reaching out to these agents.

Keep It Real

In the space below write your cover letter and the plan that will set you apart when you request meetings with prospective agents:

Notes

CLASS 1: THE BUSINESS OF ACTING

The Agency Interview

Before you watch Video 14 — The Agency Interview

People give all sorts of conflicting advice about how to act in different sorts of interviews. What, if anything, have you heard about interviewing with a potential agent? Even if you haven't heard anything, what sort of feelings does the thought of interviewing with an agent bring up? Be aware of who's actually in charge of the interview.

Watch Video 14: The Agency Interview

While you watch the video:

If you've never had an agency interview, this series of videos definitely will be informative and eye-opening. And, if you have agency interview experience, you'll be able to see whether or not to make changes to your approach.

Take note of what stands out to you the first time you watch this video. Is there any advice that stands out to you because it's helpful, counter-intuitive, or not to be forgotten?

After you watch the video:

Keep It Real

Judy Kain makes it very clear you need to have talking points ready before you walk through the door—you need to drive the interview and show your personality. Prepare the following prompts; they will help you to be confident and on top of the interview when you walk into the room:

★ What's something you're able to talk about easily and effortlessly for hours?

★ Tell a story from your resume. Judy Kain recommends starting with this, "You might notice on my resume that I..."

★ Make a list of ten different types you can play, memorize them, and be ready to rattle them off to your prospective agent during the interview.

1.
2.
3.
4.
5.
6.
7.
8.
9.
10.

★ Practice asking, "If you were to represent me, how would you submit me? I see myself as... " (*then mention ten types your created above*)

★ At the close of the inteview be sure to ask, "How would you like me to follow up?"

CLASS 1: THE BUSINESS OF ACTING

Self-Taping

Before you watch Video 15 — Self-Taping Part A

The digital age is more and more about taping your own audition and sending it off to the director and producer. This does *not* mean sending a home-made video you shot on your iPad.

Watch Video 15: Self-Taping Part A

After you watch the video:

The disadvantage in self-taping is not being able to meet and charm the director. List two advantages:

1.

2.

For several important reasons, Judy Kain suggests taping at a taping facility. Why is this a better choice than taping at home?

Define "good lighting," as requested by the casting notes.

A strong reader ideally is a professional actor, not a friend or family member. Explain why you need a professional. Should they have a mic, and why?

Keep It Real

Always submit your tape early!

Before you watch Video 15 — Self-Taping Part B

Do you have an audition coach on your team?

If "no," why not?

Watch Video 15: Self-Taping Part B

After you watch the video:

You will start shooting closeup on your face and zoom out for the slate; This may include more than just stating your name. What else might the casting notes request?

An audition coach is worth the investment. Explain why.

ALWAYS provide your audition coach with which materials?

Keep It Real

Work with professionals to shoot, coach, and read with you, and you'll have a competitive and bookable audition tape. Have you ever had an audition that would have been improved with professional help?

CLASS 1: THE BUSINESS OF ACTING

SlateShots℠

Before you watch Video 16 — SlateShots℠

How many current headshots do you have?

Do you have any matching SlateShots℠ or short videos? Do your outfits match what you wore in the headshots?

Watch Video 16: Slate Shots℠

After you watch the video:

SlateShots℠ are affordable, seven-second video versions of headshots, allowing casting to hear as well as see actors. SlateShots move you to the front of the pack and they're worth the minimal investment. Make sure you create them professionally and shoot a matching SlateShot for each of your head shots.

Keep It Real

List three positive things about including SlateShots in your marketing tool kit:

1.

2.

3.

When you shoot your SlateShot℠, match the outfit and the branding to the headshot. Make the most of the seven seconds you're given to say more than just your name.

Headshot Description	Words to say during SlateShot℠ taping
Sample: Judy: Outdoorsy, fit woman in a hiking outfit	Hi, I'm Judy and I just climbed Kilimanjaro!

CLASS 1: THE BUSINESS OF ACTING

Social Media – The New Calling Card

Before you watch Video 17 – Social Media – The New Calling Card

List every social media platform you use, whether personal or professional:

Platform	Profile Name	# of Followers
LinkedIn		
Instagram		
Facebook		
You Tube		
Twitter		
TikTok		
Snapchat		

Watch Video 17: Social Media – The New Calling Card

After you watch the video:

Your presence on social media is important, but how well you promote your brand is even more vital because *everything* you post becomes part of your marketing. Are you making the most of this powerful tool?

Guidelines for using social media. Jot down an idea or note with each to help make each more effective for you:

★ Use your name, not a high school nickname, and be consistent.

★ Add your current headshots.

★ Flesh out your profile

★ Link all your acting sites

★ Mention your general geographic region, no specifics.

★ Get comfortable with the platforms.

★ Find friends outside the industry.

★ Find your voice in social media.

★ Rather than only a simple "like", engage with a written comment.

★ Be social. Target a few people and look at their friends. Find actors' sites.

Keep It Real

Build Your Brand. Post on your interests, hobbies, and work. Give insights into yourself. What's your focus?

Congratulating people is *always* a good way to engage; respond when others congratulate you. Use words, not just emojis.

CLASS 1: THE BUSINESS OF ACTING

About Judy Kain

My name is Judy Kain, actress, owner of **Keep it Real Acting Studios**, teacher, and author of *I Booked It: The Commercial Actor's Handbook*.

I recently filmed *The Business of Acting*. It's the inspiration for this workbook and for the four-part video workshop, *Inside the Business of Show*. Together they are designed to make you industry-savvy and to give you some in-depth career direction by showing you the world in which an actor maneuvers in order to get work in a very competitive industry.

Highlights:
– 40 years as a professional actress
– 400+ commercials
– Appeared in *Mad Men, This Is Us, Modern Family, The Middle, Bones, NCIS, Jane the Virgin, Seinfeld*
– "Best Casting Director Workshop in LA" twice
– Keep It Real Acting Studios (classes)
– "Favorite On-Camera Commercial Teacher in LA" four times

I've been a professional actress for 40 years, appearing in hundreds of commercials and film and television roles. My credits include a SAG-award-winning recurring role on the Emmy-winning show *Mad Men* as Olive Healey (Peggy's secretary). Other recurring credits include *Odd Couple* with Matthew Perry, *Hand of God* with Ron Pearlman, *The Fosters, For Your Love, Grosse Pointe*, and *Manhattan, AZ* with Chad Everett. I've also done numerous guest appearances on hit shows: *This Is Us, Modern Family, The Middle, Bones, NCIS, Jane the Virgin* and many more. I have more than 400 commercial credits, which include several career highlights.

As a teacher, I've transformed the careers of countless actors through my two schools. I co-founded **Talent To Go**, a training company that won "The Best Casting Director Workshop in L.A." award in 2009 and 2010. I continued my teaching legacy and success when I opened **Keep It Real Acting Studios** in 2012, an award-winning full-service acting studio that offers commercial and theatrical classes for all levels of students. I was voted *Backstage West's* "Favorite On-Camera Commercial Teacher in L.A." in 2010, 2011, 2012 and 2015. Several of our classes have also won *Backstage West's* "Favorite in LA" awards, and the school continues to produce amazing results for our students.

CLASS 2

The Castable Actor
with Tom Burke

Notes

CLASS 2: THE CASTABLE ACTOR

Are You Castable

Before you watch Video 1 — Are You Castable

What is your definition of "castable."

Watch Video 1: Are You Castable

After you watch the video:

What's the difference between being talented and being castable?

Why do you think your "bad and ugly" might help you get a job and build a career?

Tom Burke says be confident, not cocky. What's the difference?

Keep It Real

Being as objective as possible, outline your acting limitations.

Notes

CLASS 2: THE CASTABLE ACTOR

Creating and Presenting a Marketable Image

Before you watch Video 2 — Creating and Presenting a Marketable Image

Do you have an issue with describing yourself as a product to be marketed? If so, please explain.

Watch Video 2: Creating and Presenting a Marketable Image

After you watch the video:

Tom Burke says, "No one is going to get you until *you* get you first." Explain:

Who are you? Write a 20-word description, including some of your physical, emotional, and mental characteristics.

Tom Burke has given you three words to etch into your brain. *Remember* them: be **HONEST, REALISTIC,** and **SPECIFIC**

Keep It Real

It's becoming clear that being generic is not a good way to market any product, including you as an actor. Do you think you're guilty of packaging yourself generically? Why or why not?

Notes

CLASS 2: THE CASTABLE ACTOR

Type

Before you watch Video 3 — Type

Do you know your type? Does it mean type of role or physical type? Explain.

Watch Video 3: Type

After you watch the video:

Let's build your type as the *camera* sees you:

Sex_____

Age range: Age up! No more than a five-year range, bracketing your real age: _____

Physical description:
Tall/average/short:

Hair/eyes:

Body type (OWN IT! What do people compliment?):

Level of attractiveness (Be specific! Be honest!):

Economic level (You can't fake your cheekbones!):

Keep It Real

So, how would the casting director describe the type that's you, to a T?

Does this make a change to how you have been or will be approaching who you are as an actor?

For today and the foreseeable future how do you feel about this being your type?

Notes

CLASS 2: THE CASTABLE ACTOR

Marketability

Before you watch Video — Marketability

Look at your headshots. What roles do you see for the person pictured there? Do the roles you are called for match that person?

Watch Video 4: Marketability

After you watch the video:

Using your casting type, let's build the categories of roles you're right for. Be specific, creating a breakdown as complete as those the casting director creates for a casting call.

Familial roles

Professional roles (include economic level)

Male/female-specific roles

Keep It Real

Will your headshots get you called in to audition for any of these roles? Are they too generic?

Notes

CLASS 2: THE CASTABLE ACTOR

Brand, Part 1

Before you watch Video 5 – Brand, Part 1

What personality traits or characteristics do you try to hide at an audition or interview? Why and how do you think it has affected advancing your career? Do you think any of these hidden traits or characteristics can be considered an asset?

Watch Video 5: Brand, Part 1

After you watch the video:

Tom Burke says you need to bring out the bad and the ugly and OWN IT! These traits add layers and make you memorable.

Make a list of positives that people see in you, in your opinion (For example, confidence, sense of humor, sweet disposition, sassiness, never-give-up attitude, sharp wit—*what*?)

Make a list of the bad and the ugly, in your opinion, that you've been trying to keep under wraps. (Perhaps your bossiness, eye-rolling, hyena-cackle laugh, crooked smile, instant snarkiness—*what*?)

Keep It Real

Don't be what you *think* they want; be your authentic self. Bring it all out, *own it*. Remember, television is reality-based. What are you going to let out and memorably leave behind in the audition studio that others don't?

Notes

CLASS 2: THE CASTABLE ACTOR

Brand, Part 2

Before you watch Video 6 — Brand, Part 2
What do you think people will remember after spending ten minutes with you?

Watch Video 6: Brand, Part 2

After you watch the video:
Ask your siblings and close friends the following and write their comments in the space below and on the facing page. Refer to these comments from time to time to remind yourself about these comments from the people who know you best:

Please describe what kind of person I am.

What bugs you the most about me?

What did I do when I was a kid that bugged you?

Now, the big question: Why will someone hire you? (What's your brand?)

Notes

CLASS 2: THE CASTABLE ACTOR

Headshots – Five Common Mistakes

Before you watch Video 7 – Headshots – Five Common Mistakes

You know headshots are an actor's #1 calling card. Grab all of yours again for the analysis we'll do after you watch the video.

Watch Video 7: Headshots – Five Common Mistakes

After you watch the video:

Four questions to ask as you analyze your headshots:

1. Do your headshots look just like you do on a good day?_____
2. Do they show your type?_____
3. Have they branded *you*?_____
4. Do they target the roles for which you are right?_____

Keep It Real

Do you truly understand where you've gone in the wrong direction with your headshots? Write it down:

Before you shoot your new headshots, remind yourself of the five common mistakes actors make with this all-important tool.

1. Don't get generic shots
2. Make sure they show different aspects of you
3. Never, never choose your own headshot
4. Barely retouch, if at all
5. Make sure you get a compatible photographer, someone with whom you are comfortable.

Notes

CLASS 2: THE CASTABLE ACTOR

Course Wrap Up, Now What?

Before you watch Video 8 — Course Wrap Up

At auditions, do you wear clothes that help you stand out from the crowd?

Watch Video 8: Course Wrap Up

After you watch the video:

This is my type:

These are the roles I'm right for:

This is my brand:

List the uniforms you need for the roles you're right for:

Keep It Real

Review your highlight reel and your headshots. Are you emphasizing your brand? Explain why or why not.

Look at your business cards and marketing materials. Do they use any of your branding words?

Tom Burke

Notes

CLASS 2: THE CASTABLE ACTOR

Castable Conclusions

Watch Video 9: Castable Conclusions

After you watch the video

Keep It Real

Tom Burke says to "fit the role onto you," and "own everything about yourself."

Think about how you've behaved when you meet your agent and when you are called into auditions.

Have you been hiding behind a generic or false front, and how?

What quirks and flaws are you going to stop hiding?

List the specific actions you will take going forward?

CLASS 2: THE CASTABLE ACTOR

About Tom Burke

After a career as a successful model in New York, Tom transitioned into an equally successful career on the west coast in commercials, feature films, and series television. He said, "There was never a door I couldn't get into. From the moment I started out, I understood that this was a business first and foremost, so I learned to package myself as a marketable image that the industry was actually buying."

When the opportunity arose to work on the other side of the camera, Tom walked through that open door again, and he developed a niche for himself as an on-set acting coach. He has worked with some of the most talented award winning actors and directors in the world, (including an academy award winner).

Tom's wealth of experience in different acting fields, together with his solid training from some of the most renowned acting teachers in New York, Chicago, and Los Angeles, have given him an uncanny ability to successfully coach a wide range of actors. His keen eye and knack for pinpointing and understanding both performers and the business, make Tom one of LA's premier image consultants and branding specialists for actors, models, and musicians. He also writes a column for *Backstage* that focuses on helping actors understand the importance of packaging their marketable, branded image.

"I have seen firsthand the unbelievable difference Tom Burke can make in someone's career. He can look at someone and know exactly what changes they need to make . . . and immediately, they go from a 'want-to-be' to a professional."

—**MM, Talent Manager**

CLASS 3

How To Break Into Broadway
with Christopher Henry Young

Notes

CLASS 3: HOW TO BREAK INTO BROADWAY

Introduction

Before you watch Video 1 – Introduction

Have you ever attended Broadway shows in person? What impressed you the most about your experience and what impact did the experience have on your life.

Watch Video 1: Introduction

After you watch the video:

What do you think Christopher means when he says "creating a path" to your career?

Keep It Real

What do you want to learn from this class? Create a *specific* goal with a timeline:

Christopher Henry Young

Notes

CLASS 3: HOW TO BREAK INTO BROADWAY

Preparation, Part One

Before you watch Video 4 — Preparation, Part One

Pull out your current headshots and acting résumé and review them.

If you don't have these necessary professional tools, why don't you?

Watch Video 4: Preparation, Part One

After you watch the video:

Headshot: Do your headshots look like an everyday, recognizable version of you, torso through head?

                 Do they show your personality?

                 Do you have both serious and joyful shots?

Résumé: Is it up to date, clear and simple, including all your performance credits? Is a headshot stapled to each résumé?

Keep It Real

Headshots: If they don't live up to Christopher's standards and you don't feel they are helping you book jobs, consider having them re-shot. Part IV of this workbook gives you an in-depth explanation of the headshot process.

Résumé: At the least, edit your current résumé. If it's cluttered or too long, rewrite it from scratch.

Notes

CLASS 3: HOW TO BREAK INTO BROADWAY

Preparation, Part Two

Before you watch Video 5 — Preparation Part Two

Do you feel prepared when you attend auditions? Why or why not?

What songs (and styles of songs) have you already prepared to sing for auditions?

What items do you bring with you to auditions?

Watch Video 5: Preparation, Part Two

After watching the video:

Create your audition book.

- ★ The book is a three-ring binder of double-sided sheet music for the accompanist, including ballad and upbeat songs in each style listed below in the Keep It Real section.

- ★ The casting notice will probably require you to prepare a "song in the style of show." Do so even if not requested.

- ★ *Only include songs you have memorized.*

- ★ Mark 16- and 32-bar cuts that include a complete section (verse, bridge, or chorus). Be prepared to sing entire song if asked.

Put together your dance bag. It will accompany you to **EVERY** audition. Include:

- ★ Audition book
- ★ Extra headshots/résumés
- ★ Dance shoes
- ★ Spare t-shirts/audition outfits
- ★ Toiletry kits
- ★ Water bottles, a high-energy snack or two.

Keep It Real

Broadway-style song categories include traditional and contemporary musical theater, pop, rock, jazz, R&B, funk, and character songs. What song styles do you think you need to work on to improve your technique?

Notes

CLASS 3: *How To Break Into Broadway*

Stage Skills

Before you watch Video 2 — Stage Skills

What skills do you think Broadway actors need to master?

_____

Watch Video 2: Stage Skills

_____
_____

After you watch the video:

Find your talents! List and assess your own stage skills.

Singing: Do you read music?

                How good is your voice? Have you had lessons and training?

                What's your classification (bass, baritone, alto, soprano, etc.)

                What vocal styles are easiest for you (hip hop, country, pop, jazz, etc.)?

Dancing: Evaluate your general dance and acrobatic skills:

                Specific types of dances you've *mastered* (Latin, ballroom, ballet, hip hop, etc.)

Other skills, such as magic/illusions, skateboarding, unicycling, puppetry, roller blades, playing musical instruments, etc.:

Keep It Real

In which of my skills can I become truly proficient with some additional training?

Notes

CLASS 3: HOW TO BREAK INTO BROADWAY

Classes and Training

Before you watch Video 3 – Classes and Training

Describe the last time you took classes or trained in specific performance skills?

How did it help you?

Watch Video 3: Classes and Training

After you watch the video:

Why do successful actors take additional classes and training?

Define the difference between:

Taking classes:

Training:

Keep It Real

What type of class or additional training do you feel would help you the most with your acting career and why?

Research two potential classes or additional training you find accessible and affordable.

Notes

CLASS 3: HOW TO BREAK INTO BROADWAY

Auditions

Before you watch Video 6 — Auditions

Are you prepared to sing, dance, *and* act in an audition? What preparations have you made in the past and how has that worked for you? How does a *professional* audition differ from others in which you have participated?

Watch Video 6: Auditions

After watching the video:

Where will you find information about upcoming auditions?

Audition/Casting Notice: These notices contain information that you need for proper preparation. List the key points:

Accompanist: When you hand your audition book to the accompanist, what additional information should you tell them?

How do you give the tempo to the accompanist?

The Audition
Why do you "act" the song?

Keep It Real

Create your *audition journal*. Buy a durable notebook; write Christopher's description of the audition process at the front of the book. You will keep your notes from every future audition in this notebook.

Christopher Henry Young

Notes

CLASS 3: *How To Break Into Broadway*

Self-Care

Before you watch Video 7 — Self-Care

As a stage actor and a physical performer all of your physical skills and attributes need to be in peak form. Think about how you currently prepare your body for auditions and what dietary disciplines you practice in order to keep yourself in the best shape possible.

Watch Video 7: Self-Care

After you watch the video:

Christopher's "proper warmup" heats up his entire body so every limb is fluid and his mind is centered. Preparing body and mind gets him ready to "dance his face off." With that in mind take note of the items below and follow up with these three very important aspects of self-care.

★ **Physical warmup**: getting you body ready to dance & protecting it from damage.

In Videos 9, 10, and 11 Christopher demonstrates the physical warm-ups he developed in order to get his body ready to perform.

★ **Vocal warmup**: important for speaking *or* singing so you can reach full vocal ability and access all notes without damage. Start mid-range to low-range, then low-range to high-range. The link below shows you some speific vocal exercises that help you warm up your voice:

https://www.musicnotes.com/now/tips/enhance-your-voice-with-these-vocal-warm-ups-and-breathing-exercises/

NOTE: If you receive a 404 error message, go to the search tool on the MusicNotes page and type, "breathing exercises".

★ **Diet**: In Video 8 Christopher talks about the importance of diet and how it relates to your ability to perform. Review Video 8 and take note of the handout on page 100 showing links to specific sites that talk about food and nutrition.

Keep It Real

Describe your diet in fewer than 20 words. Do you think there is room for improvement?

Notes

CLASS 3: HOW TO BREAK INTO BROADWAY

Nutritional Approach to a Broadway Body

Before you watch Video 8 — Nutritional Approach to a Broadway Body

Describe your current diet and, if you can, esitmate your daily coloric intake and how many calories you burn during a day.

Watch Video 8: Nutritional Approach to a Broadway Body

After you watch the video:

Whether you are performing in rehearsals, a running show, workshops, or a series of auditions high-protein, high-energy meals and snacks are recommended in order to keep you fueled, ready to perform, and to use your energy to its fullest potential.

If you don't already have an appropriate "Broadway Diet", review the links Christopher Henry Young recommends on the next page. They will help you find a healthy, nutritional approach that's right for you. Load the links into your phone and use them as a quick reference source.

Keep It Real

If you think your diet needs to be improved review the links on page 100 and start to make some revisions. Revisit this page and video in a month or two and describe your progress and the changes you've made to your nutritional habits.

Below are Christopher Henry Young's website suggestions to help you find a nutritional dietary approach that works for you.

IDEAL MEAL PLAN

https://www.livestrong.com/article/443807-ideal-meal-plan/

HEALTHY FOODS FOR DANCERS

https://www.liveabout.com/healthy-diet-for-dancers-1006899

HEALTHY SNACK OPTIONS

https://www.pointemagazine.com/healthy-food-for-dancers-2565527028.html

FITNESS, HEALTH, NUTRITION

FitForBroadway has tons of blog posts about Fitness, Health, Nutrition and all things about Broadway Bodies!

https://www.fitforbroadway.com/

CLASS 3: HOW TO BREAK INTO BROADWAY

At-Home Warm-Up, Section 1, Cardio

Before you watch Video 9 — At-Home Warm-Up, Section 1, Cardio

You need to warm-up your body before you stretch and before you do any performance or audition. To practice this, find a spot in your home that has space for your extended body and outstretched arms and legs whether you're doing jumping jacks or planks. Remove anything within reach of your waving hands and extended legs that could be damaged. When you start doing these exercises, it's helpful to see yourself in the mirror or have someone observe you to make sure your techniques are good.

Put on comfortable workout clothes and athletic shoes. Yes, Christopher is going to have you perform every one of his customized at-home warmup exercises right now. Prepare to get your heart rate up!

Watch Video 9: At-Home Warm-Up Exercises, Section 1, Cardio; Raise your heart rate and body heat

While you watch the video:

Stop and replay it as often as necessary to grasp both his techniques and his safety concerns. Watch for the extensions and positions Christopher demonstrates when as he moves through the exercises. Doing all movements properly will make you loose and flexible, not just sweaty and tired.

★ **Jumping jacks: 20 reps.** Christopher has a light-footed, elegant style of jumping jacks, springing his legs out wider than shoulders, touching hands at the top, using precise movements and full extensions. He keeps his chest high and chin forward as he jumps. How springy, fully extended, and light are you?

★ **Squat jacks: 10 reps.** This movement combines basic squat and the "legs together" position of the jumping jack. Squat, head up, wide stance, toes pointed out, chest stays up. Make sure your knees don't go in front of your toes and your rear end goes back where it should be. Spring upright into legs-together position. That's one rep.

★ **Butterfly jacks: 20 reps.** You want to be as light-footed and fully extended as you are with the jumping jacks, just on a horizontal plane rather than a vertical one. Keep arms level!

Keep It Real

As a dancing, singing Broadway actor, you have to be in incredible shape. Were you short of breath after doing 50 reps and getting your heart rate up? Would you have been able to sing, smile, and dance at that moment?

Notes

CLASS 3: HOW TO BREAK INTO BROADWAY

At-Home Warm-Up, Sections 2 & 3, Joints

Before you watch Video 10 — At-Home Warm-Up, Sections 2 & 3, Joints

You need to warm-up your body before you stretch and before you do any performance or audition. Find a spot in your home that has space for your extended body and outstretched arms and legs whether you're doing jumping jacks or planks. Remove anything within reach of your waving hands and extended legs that could be damaged. When you start doing these exercises, it's helpful to see yourself in the mirror or have someone observe you to make sure your techniques are good.

Put on comfortable workout clothes and athletic shoes. Yes, Christopher is going to have you perform every one of his customized at-home warmup exercises right now. Prepare to get your heart rate up!

Watch Video 10: At-Home Warm-Up Exercises, Sections 2 & 3, Joints
Loosen your joints and protect them from damage

While you watch the video:

Stop and replay it as often as necessary to grasp both his techniques and his safety concerns. Watch for the extensions and positions Christopher demonstrates when as he moves through the exercises. Doing all movements properly will make you loose and flexible, not just sweaty and tired.

- ★ **Wrists and shoulders, 20 reps.** Stretch both arms in front of you and hold them still. Rotate wrists in a circular motion to the outside, and then to the inside. Rotate your shoulders in a circle from front to back, then back to front. That's one rep.
- ★ **Ankles, 10 reps.**
    - Keeping toe of right foot on the ground, roll ankle in a complete clockwise circle, allowing your knee to swivel out as you rotate. Repeat counterclockwise.
    - Lift your right heel, bending your right knee slightly, and press down into the arch of your foot. Repeat with left foot. That's one rep.

- ★ **Head-neck/chest/hips, 5 reps.** Do these exercises in sequence, flowing from one to another.
  - **Head and neck.** Take a count of eight to complete each controlled, slow rotation. Put your chin down, use the top of your head to circle over your right shoulder and around 360 degrees, looking up and back as your head swivels around, then over your left shoulder to the front. (Do not lean your head too far back.) Swivel your head slowly in the opposite location..
  - **Chest.** Taking a count of four to complete the rotation on each side, slowly draw a figure eight by swiveling your shoulders, moving up and down as well as front to back and side to side.
  - **Hips.** Taking a count of two to complete the movement, circle your hips clockwise. Repeat counterclockwise.

Lower Body — Strong hips, legs, and glutes carry your body weight

- ★ **Squats, 15 reps.** A slow and controlled movement with a wide stance, feet outside hips, toes pointed out, knees over toes, chest up, head up, rear end back.

- ★ **Squats with toe taps, 15 reps.** Squat; when you're lowered, reach your right leg straight back and touch your toe to the ground. Repeat on left side. That's one rep.

Keep It Real

Flexible joints are less likely to be injured; injuries are the bane of dancers' lives. Evaluate your flexibility honestly. If you're not as flexible as you know you need to be, commit to doing these exercises daily.

Notes

CLASS 3: HOW TO BREAK INTO BROADWAY

At-Home Warm-Up, Sections 4 & 5, Core

Before you watch Video 11 – At-Home Warm-Up, Sections 4 & 5, Core

You need to warm-up your body before you stretch and before you do any performance or audition. Find a spot in your home that has space for your extended body and outstretched arms and legs whether you're doing jumping jacks or planks. Remove anything within reach of your waving hands and extended legs that could be damaged. When you start doing these exercises, it's helpful to see yourself in the mirror or have someone observe you to make sure your techniques are good.

Put on comfortable workout clothes and athletic shoes. Yes, Christopher is going to have you perform every one of his customized at-home warmup exercises right now. Prepare to get your heart rate up!

Watch Video 11: At-Home Warm-Up Exercises, Sections 4 & 5, Core

While you watch the video:

Stop and replay it as often as necessary to grasp both his techniques and his safety concerns. Watch for the extensions and positions Christopher wants when you jump, squat, toe-tap, and move through the exercises. Doing all movements properly will make your muscles and limbs loose and flexible, not just sweaty and tired.

A strong, flexible core is key to every move you make on stage.

- ★ **Basic plank.** Palms directly under shoulders, body straight. Don't sag; engage your core muscles. Hold 45-60 seconds, depending upon your fitness level.

- ★ **Plank with shoulder taps, 5 reps.** Do basic plank, but widen your legs for stability; go to your knees if you need to. Keep weight on left hand and your body as level as possible as you lift right hand to your left shoulder. Repeat with other side. That's one rep.

Upper body – Loose arms and shoulders relax you and look graceful

★ **Arms and wrists.** Rotate your right arm back straight from the shoulder in a complete circle while rotating wrist out in its own smaller circle. Next, rotate your right arm forward as you rotate wrist inward. Do a controlled full rotation. Repeat with your left arm. That's one rep.

★ **Shoulder and chest stretch, 5 or more reps.** Stretch out your right arm, continue to move it across your chest to your left. Bending your left arm at the elbow, lift up your left fist, trap your right arm, and pull it in against your chest. Squeeze. Repeat with other arm. That's one rep.

Keep It Real

Musical theater, in particular, requires a level of physical fitness and endurance far more demanding than most aspiring actors realize. These basic warm-up exercises are just that; they're no substitute for a well-balanced and executed fitness regime. If you're not working out regularly, *start now!*

Notes

CLASS 3: HOW TO BREAK INTO BROADWAY

You Booked A Show, Now What

Before you watch Video 12 – You Booked A Show, Now What

If you have been a cast member, think about the experience and how you and others in the cast reacted to the process — from first rehearsal to the opening of the show.

If you never had a cast experience think about your expectations.

Watch Video 12: Your Booked A Show, Now What

While you watch the video:

Make a mental note of anything you're hearing or learning about for the first time.

After you watch the video:

To prepare for rehearsals the creative team likely will deliver three pertinent materials to the cast; can you list what they are?

During the rehearsal process Christopher Henry Young keeps what he call his "show bible". What does he track with it and how does it help him during the long process?

During this segment the following three roles of every production are discussed; can you explain their purpose:

★ Swing

★ Standby

★ Understudy

Keep It Real

On your path to Broadway do you think adding the roles of swing, standby, or understudy to your reume' will have an impact on your career; why?

Christopher Henry Young

Notes

CLASS 3: HOW TO BREAK INTO BROADWAY

Professionalism

Before you watch Video 13 — Professionalism

Are you always on time and well-prepared for scheduled events?

Define "professionalism" as you think it applies to an acting career.

Watch Video 13: Professionalism

After you watch the video:

List three ways you can be prepared for auditions and rehearsals:

Christopher leaves some of the details about the following methods of showing professionalism up to you. Do some research with other actors, or reflect on your own experiences, then jot down a few words of explanation:

★ Respect other actors' process and aid in a safe process

★ Adhere to rehearsal etiquette

★ Accept notes from the creative team

★ Always be fully invested and bring your full energy

Keep It Real

"Notes" from the creative team means feedback on your performance and/or instructions for doing it again, probably differently from the way you envisioned. Are you easily able to listen, smile, not disagree, accept, and move straight into a different performance? How easily have you done that in the past? How can you make this a more positive experience?

Notes

CLASS 3: HOW TO BREAK INTO BROADWAY

Equity and Non-Equity

Before you watch Video 9 — Equity and Non-Equity

Define a workers' union.

Why are pension plans and work safety part of a union's function?

Watch Video 9: Equity and Non-Equity

After you watch the video:

The Actors' Equity Association (Equity) was established in 1913, and it represents only live theatrical performers. Go to their website, https://www.actorsequity.org/ and research their various memberships, fees, and dues.

Equity reaches beyond Broadway. In addition to Disneyworld, what theatrical venues are reserved for Equity actors?

Can non-union actors work in theatre?

Name another well-known actors' union.

Keep It Real

What are some of the benefits of joining Equity?

What are the disadvantages?

Christopher Henry Young

Notes

CLASS 3: HOW TO BREAK INTO BROADWAY

Common Mistakes

Before you watch Video 15 – Common Mistakes

What characteristics do you have that make you stand out in a crowd of actors?

Watch Video 15: Common Mistakes

After you watch the video:

Representation: Christopher recommends waiting until you're established before you hire an agent or manager.

List two reasons why you should wait:

1.

2.

Have you used an online audition hub yet? Why not? Research them and jot down two you will use:

1.

2.

Don't copy anyone. Expand on the exercise you did prior to watching the video:

★ What are the detailed specifics about your unique characteristics? Do you have extra zip in your movements, a wild and crazy grin, a nose like Cyrano's, expressive hands, a rasp in your voice, a gangly walk, huge, sad eyes? Be as descriptive as possible.

★ What is your rarest quality or feature, something you don't see at in other actors? How can you emphasize it?

Keep It Real

Avoid any tendency to blend in with the crowd or copy a successful performer. Cultivate your unique qualities and characteristics that helps you stand out from the rest.

Notes

CLASS 3: HOW TO BREAK INTO BROADWAY

Career Longevity

Before you watch Video 16 — Career Longevity

Do you have extra pressure or criticism in your life right now? Describe it and how it's affecting your career.

Watch Video 16: Career Longevity

After you watch the video:

Continue to grow. The theater world is evolving. Always keep training; be prepared. Are you signed up for classes and workshops? Where and when?

Show the best version of yourself. Christopher says to let your talent speak loudly on your behalf. Use everything you have, including your looks. Remind yourself of your skills and acting/dancing/singing chops. List at least five.

1.

2.

3.

4.

5.

Clear your life of anything that's not serving your goal. Look at the full picture; how can you deflect/get rid of the pressure or criticism you described above? Get rid of the extra clutter, both physical and emotional. Look at the full picture and give yourself your best chance.

Don't end your career prematurely. Don't push past your limits. Keep your muscles and voice ready and as resilient and healthy as possible? Do you know what your limits are?

Keep It Real

Don't let what happens today damage your future. Keep calm and collected.

Notes

CLASS 3: HOW TO BREAK INTO BROADWAY

Course Wrap-Up and Conclusions

Watch Video 17: Course Wrap-up and Conclusions

After you watch the video:

Christopher Henry Young says, "Grow and keep learning. Always be a student of the craft!

★ What are your next steps forward on your acting path?

★ Sign up for a class that stresses the performance skills on which you need to work?

★ Participate in a workshop. Research at least two accessible workshops for additional training.

★ Continue to prepare the audition tools he's recommended. Periodically update your notes in Lesson 10 until the tools are complete. Keep them updated.

★ Communicate with other actors. Research and join social organizations, guilds, professional groups (list at least two you will join). Read blogs, follow social media. Go to performances!

★ Go to casting calls. Go to auditions. DON'T LET UP! Break a leg!

Notes

CLASS 3: HOW TO BREAK INTO BROADWAY

About Christopher Henry Young

Born in Baltimore, Maryland and raised in York, Pennsylvania, Christopher danced, sang in church and school choirs, played sports, and entertained his family with goofy reenactments of his favorite cartoon characters. At 14, he auditioned for his high school's production of Disney's *Beauty and the Beast*. "Something about the lyrics in that show spoke to me. I mean, who doesn't feel misunderstood as a teenager; but, I connected with that story."

As he learned to empathize with characters and to understand the excitement and adventure within the roles, Christopher fell in love with theatre. "Going from *Rent* to *Peter Pan*, *Crazy For You* to *Les Misérables*, theatre was the way I learned to understand and express my feelings and emotions. Learning to see life through another human's eyes changed how I saw the world of the characters in plays and musicals."

Making his professional debut in *TAP: The Show*, a Matt Davenport Production at Hershey Park, Christopher began to learn everything that being a professional performer involves. Both at Hershey Park and later with Carnival Cruise lines, Christopher interacted face-to-face with many of the audience members. "Performing shows designed to break the fourth wall was exactly what I dreamed of doing. Getting to make the audience part of the experience and see their journey as you perform your heart out is like nothing else imaginable."

During his four years with Carnival Cruise lines, Christopher worked with forward-thinking artists and performers from all over the world, learning from them and growing as an artist. His special skillset grew, and in addition to singing, acting, and dancing (from hip hop and tap to ballroom), he added basic silk/aerial rope training, basic combat training, puppetry skills, and choreography.

After moving to New York City, Christopher began his first regional theatre contract across the country with the Oregon Shakespeare Festival. And, during two seasons in regional theatre, he had roles in a wide variety of productions including *Guys & Dolls* (Mary Zimmerman, director), *The Wiz* (Robert O'Hara, director), *The Winter's Tale* (Desdemona Chiang, director), and the world premiere of *Head Over Heels*.

Returning to New York, Christopher joined the production of *A Bronx Tale: The Musical* and he helped to launch a developmental workshop for a new musical about the Temptations, the musical group that helped him find his own voice. His partner in the workshop was Sergio Trujillo, choreographer of *On Your Feet*, *Memphis*, and *A Bronx Tale: The Musical*.

Currently Christopher is appearing in *Hamilton* in San Francisco.

CLASS 4

The Castable Headshot
with Tom Burke & Kevin McIntyre

Notes

CLASS 4: THE CASTABLE HEADSHOT

Know Who You Are

Before you watch Video 1 — Know Who You Are

Know who you are doesn't mean *where you come* from or your background—it means understanding what *castable type* you are, your *brand*, and what theatrical and advertising *roles* you are right for.

Keep It Real

Describe your castable type and brand.

Watch Video 1: Know Who You Are

After you watch the video:

What roles are you right for?

1.

2.

3.

4.

What's your shot list for these roles? What look do you want for each of the roles?

1.

2.

3.

4.

Build the wardrobe (uniform) for each role, not limited to what's in your closet. Remember, the shots are thumbnails, and you're competing among 3,000 others to be called.

1.

2.

3.

4.

What *range* are you bringing to each shot? Which aspect of your personality, your brand, works best? You want different personalities to show.

1.

2.

3.

4.

CLASS 4: THE CASTABLE HEADSHOT

Finding a Photographer

Before you watch Video 2 — Finding a Photographer

Review the last time you had a headshot session. How well did you get along with the photographer?

What stood out about *their* personality and technique?

Keep It Real

Did they capture *your* brand and personality? How?

Watch Video 2: Finding a Photographer

After you watch the video:

Ask yourself these questions to calculate your comfort level with circumstances and photographers:

Would you go to their apartment?

Would you get into a car with them?

Are you okay changing clothes in public?

Are you more comfortable shooting with a photographer of the same sex or different sex?

List four contacts whom you'll ask for photographer referrals:

1.

2.

3.

4.

Questions to ask them:

Why are they on your referral list?

How long have you had them there?

Would you work with them again?

What was it like working with them?

Where did they shoot, street/studio/apartment?

How did you feel?

Are the shots working, getting you booked?

Tip: Make sure the photographer can shoot your physical type/ethnicity, showing who you are.

CLASS 4: THE CASTABLE HEADSHOT

The Cost of Your Headshot Session

Before you watch Video 3 — The Cost of Your Headshot Session

What have you budgeted for your shots?

What did you spend on your last headshots?

Keep It Real

Did they get you auditions and bookings and how?

Watch Video 3: The Cost of Your Headshot Session

After you watch the video:

Research the range of headshot prices in your area.

Photographer #1 _____

Price range

Photographer #2 _____

Price range

Photographer #3 _____

Price range

Notes

CLASS 4: THE CASTABLE HEADSHOT

Bring Emotion to Your Headshot Session

Before you watch Video 4 — Bring Emotion to Your Headshot Session

Review the headshots you've designed for your shoot.

Watch Video 4: Bring Emotion to Your Headshot Session

After you watch the video:

Each shot should be treated like a separate acting scene. You need to bring out innate emotion to the camera for each shot.

How do you see each type of shot? Who do you see facing you, inside the camera, who brings the emotion out? What do they say to you? What do you want to say to them?

Write down the dialog for each of your four headshots; do your best to bring *you* out.

1. Dialogue:

   How will you describe this shot to your photographer?

2. Dialogue:

   How will you describe this shot to your photographer?

3. Dialogue:

   How will you describe this shot to your photographer?

4. Dialogue:

   How will you describe this shot to your photographer?

Notes

CLASS 4: THE CASTABLE HEADSHOT

What Makes a Good and a Bad Headshot?

Before you watch Video 5 – What Makes a Good and a Bad Headshot?

Describe what you think is considered a good headshot.

Watch Video 5: What Makes a Good and a Bad Headshot?

After you watch the video:

How do you want to change your description of a good headshot?

Do the headshots you're planning set you apart and show your range?

Do they qualify as a "portfolio" and why?

How do you plan to make your connection with the camera?

Keep It Real

What helps you avoid making a bad headshot, other than technical mistakes?

Notes

CLASS 4: THE CASTABLE HEADSHOT

Q&A From the Photographer's Viewpoint

Before you watch Video 6 — Q&A From the Photographer's Viewpoint

Think back to your last headshot session and focus on the interaction you had with your photographer before, during, and after the session. Based on the work you booked using the headshots from that session, write down how the session could have gone differently.

Watch Video 6: Q&A From the Photographer's Viewpoint

After you watch the video:

What are the most important issues to discuss with your photographer?

What are some good reasons for giving them your old headshots?

Keep It Real

What's the most common way actors sabotage their own shoot?

Notes

CLASS 4: THE CASTABLE HEADSHOT

Arrive at the Studio

Before you watch Video 7 — Arrive at the Studio

Who's in charge at a shoot, the photographer or the actor; and why?

Do you think it's better to do your own hair and makeup or to have it done professionally; why or why not?

Watch Video 7: Arrive at the Studio

After you watch the video:

Review:

When you arrive acclimate yourself to the studio, get comfortable

Meet the photographer, have some brief small talk to get to know each other and to feel comfortable with them

Relax

Bring out the uniforms; keep some options to get input on color, etc.

Bring some makeup variations with you—different lipsticks, etc.

Keep It Real

If you're not great at doing your own hair and makeup, **learn how**! It'll help you not only at headshot shoots but you'll find it to be invaluable at auditions.

Notes

CLASS 4: THE CASTABLE HEADSHOT

Headshot Session Demonstration

Before watching Video 8 — Headshot Session Demonstration
Who runs the session, the actor or the photographer?

Watch Video 8: Headshot Session Demonstration

After you watch the video:

REVIEW:

   Deep breaths.

   Connect into the center of the lens.

   Take one last look in the mirror and leave it there. Don't worry about how you look.

   Connecting with the camera is your only concern.

   If the light's too bright or you're uncomfortable, LET THEM KNOW.

   If you need a moment, ask.

   Take a wide stance and plant yourself.

   Stop talking! You're there to do a job, comfortable but focused.

   Tell the photographer about the scenarios you have prepared. They will help you get there.

   Do something with your hands—touch your ring or your fingernails.

   Chin down; you're not on stage.

Notes

CLASS 4: THE CASTABLE HEADSHOT

Now What? Post-Headshot Session Process

Before you watch Video 9 — Now What? Post-Headshot Session Process

Keep It Real

Are you absolutely positive about your type? What is it? You need to know in order to evaluate your headshots.

Watch Video 9: Now What? Post-Headshot Session Process

After you watch the video:

What do you know about:

★ Color correction?

★ Other editing that the photographer may do?

★ Retouching?

Are you prepared for Dropbox or other electronic delivery of your shots?

Look at the shots when they arrive and walk away for a day or so. When you go back to your shots who will help you choose the ones you want?

Put up fifteen different pictures on social media, get feedback, then pick a shot or two from each look. Which social media will you use?

What is better than looking exactly like your headshots?

Notes

CLASS 4: THE CASTABLE HEADSHOT

About Tom Burke and About Kevin McIntyre

Tom Burke

After a career as a successful model in New York, Tom transitioned into an equally successful career on the west coast in commercials, feature films, and series television. He said, "There was never a door I couldn't get into. From the moment I started out, I understood that this was a business first and foremost, so I learned to package myself as a marketable image that the industry was actually buying."

When the opportunity arose to work on the other side of the camera, Tom walked through that open door again, and he developed a niche for himself as an on-set acting coach. He has worked with some of the most talented award winning actors and directors in the world. (For more about Tom go to page 81)

Kevin McIntyre

Kevin McIntyre's background as a successful actor and musical performer gives him an edge as a headshot photographer. He's performed leading roles in many musicals across Canada and the US, including *Miss Saigon* (original Canadian cast), *Les Misérables, Forever Plaid, Mamma Mia* and *The Addams Family*. He has also worked in many national commercials, and continues to perform in concert as a singer and bagpiper throughout the US, Canada, and the U.K.

He says, "As a performer, I see headshots in a different way. I know how important it is to have a shot that works and gets you in the door."

He's been a photographer in Los Angeles for nearly 24 years, specializing in natural-light photography. In addition to his studio in downtown LA, he owns a studio in Canada, where he works with actors in the Canadian market. His notable clients include Oscar winners Octavia Spenser and Mo'nique, as well as Ken Jeong, Eva Mendes, and Kendall Jenner. Kevin ensures his clients get a portfolio showing their range and clarifying their brand to maximize their impact on online casting sites. His unique understanding of actors' needs helps him connect with his clients and bring out the best in their shots. Clients leave his studios confident they'll have headshots that work for them.

www.ingramcontent.com/pod-product-compliance
Lightning Source LLC
Chambersburg PA
CBHW081013040426
42444CB00014B/3193